Astrological Hemp

Astrological Hemp

Matthew Petchinsky

Astrological Hemp: Aligning the Stars with Earth's Ancient Herb

By: Matthew Petchinsky

Introduction: A Cosmic Connection Reawakened

Throughout history, humanity has turned both upward and downward in search of answers. The stars above served as calendars, omens, and mirrors for the soul, while the plants below offered nourishment, medicine, and spiritual communion. Among the most powerful allies from the natural world is hemp—a resilient, healing plant used by countless cultures for physical wellness and ceremonial purposes. Likewise, astrology, the ancient language of the stars, has guided civilizations for millennia in understanding cycles, personality, and fate. *Astrological Hemp* emerges at the intersection of these two timeless forces, offering a harmonious roadmap to deeper self-awareness and holistic well-being.

This book reawakens a forgotten synergy—one that bridges the celestial and terrestrial, the intuitive and the physical. It invites you to explore how the rhythmic dance of planets and signs affects your body, mood, and energy flow—and how hemp can help you align with these celestial movements. When we understand our astrological blueprint and attune our self-care to the stars, we begin to live in accordance with our cosmic design. When we add hemp—an ancient and adaptive botanical remedy—we ground that understanding into daily life, ritual, and healing practice.

Both astrology and hemp are now enjoying powerful resurgences in modern society. No longer dismissed as fringe or folklore, these tools are being re-integrated into science, wellness, and spiritual lifestyles. Astrology is used by psychologists, CEOs, and therapists alike to uncover patterns and support personal development. Hemp, with its non-psychoactive compound CBD and richly beneficial terpene profiles, is championed for reducing anxiety, inflammation, and stress while improving sleep, mood, and emotional resilience.

Together, these two systems create a bridge between cosmic influence and earth-based healing.

This book is for anyone seeking:

- **Personalized wellness based on your birth chart.**
- **Natural methods for emotional regulation and physical healing.**
- **Daily and seasonal rituals that combine celestial events with herbal support.**
- **A deeper connection to the rhythms of nature and your own inner universe.**

Whether you're a beginner to astrology, a curious explorer of plant medicine, or someone craving a deeper ritualistic connection to life, *Astrological Hemp* will guide you through every zodiac sign, planetary event, and cosmic season—pairing each with mindful hemp practices that restore harmony to your body, mind, and spirit.

You'll discover how to:

- Align with your Sun, Moon, and Rising sign for better mental and physical wellness.
- Use hemp to navigate Mercury retrogrades, eclipses, and other cosmic turbulence.
- Enhance spiritual practices like journaling, meditation, and lunar rituals.
- Tailor hemp use based on the changing solar seasons and lunar phases.
- Create your own rituals based on planetary movements and energetic needs.

As you journey through the pages, you'll be invited to reconnect with the ancient rhythms that have always been available—those of the sky and the soil. In a world that often feels fragmented and rushed, this book offers a slow, cyclical path back to wholeness. It is a reawakening of the bond between star and seed, planet and plant, intention and healing.

Welcome to the cosmic garden. Your personalized path to balance begins here. ◈◈

Chapter 1: Astrology and Hemp — An Ancient Union

Across civilizations and centuries, humans have sought connection—with nature, with the stars, and with themselves. While modern society often separates science from spirituality and medicine from mysticism, the ancient world embraced an integrative approach. Two of the oldest tools used for healing, insight, and self-alignment were the heavens above and the herbs below. Among the most revered: astrology and hemp.

This chapter uncovers the rich, interconnected history of these two traditions—how they shaped civilizations, symbolized deeper wisdom, and why their modern-day revival marks a return to ancient, sustainable truth.

◈ The Birth of Astrology: Mapping Meaning in the Sky

Long before telescopes and modern astronomy, our ancestors looked to the stars not just for navigation, but for guidance. The Babylonians were among the first to develop a structured astrological system over 4,000 years ago. They tracked planetary movements and lunar cycles, associating them with earthly events like harvests, floods, and the fate of rulers. These observations laid the groundwork for what would become the zodiac.

In Egypt, astrology was interwoven with medicine, temple practices, and governance. Pharaohs consulted star priests, who used celestial alignments to dictate sacred rituals and public decisions. The Greeks later refined astrology into a symbolic framework for personality and destiny, with thinkers like Ptolemy formalizing astrological philosophy into enduring texts.

Across India, China, Mesoamerica, and the Middle East, different forms of celestial mapping emerged. In each, the stars were not inert specks of light—they were divine storytellers, cosmic clocks, and energetic indicators of personal and planetary health.

◈ The Legacy of Hemp: Medicine, Ritual, and Utility

Simultaneously, hemp was being cultivated and revered across continents. Archaeological evidence shows hemp fiber was used in China as early as 8,000 BCE. Ancient texts from the Chinese pharmacopeia describe its use for easing pain, calming the spirit, and enhancing meditative states.

In India, hemp was sacred to Shiva and incorporated into Ayurvedic medicine to treat anxiety, digestion issues, and insomnia. Bhang—a cannabis-infused drink—was consumed in religious festivals and spiritual ceremonies to open the mind and connect with the divine.

Egyptian papyri refer to cannabis extracts used in healing salves, while Greek physicians like Dioscorides and Galen praised it for its ability to soothe pain and inflammation. In the Islamic Golden Age, hemp derivatives were included in medical texts, and in medieval Europe, monks grew hemp in monastery gardens for textiles, paper, and medicinal poultices.

Hemp's enduring power lies in its versatility: food, fiber, medicine, spiritual sacrament. It was considered both sacred and utilitarian—a plant that nourished both body and soul.

◈ Symbolic Parallels: Above and Below

Astrology and hemp share more than antiquity; they mirror each other symbolically.

- **Astrology** represents the unseen forces—energetic patterns, archetypes, and potentialities. It teaches that what is above reflects what is below.
- **Hemp** offers grounding—it is a physical, earthy conduit for healing and nervous system regulation. It helps us embody those cosmic insights in our daily lives.

Both systems promote **balance, awareness**, and **resonance with natural rhythms**. While astrology maps the soul's blueprint, hemp helps soothe the body's reactions to stress, misalignment, and disconnection. Together, they form a bridge between the metaphysical and the material.

◈ Suppression and Separation in the Modern Age

As the world transitioned through colonization, industrialization, and the rise of mechanistic science, both astrology and hemp were marginalized. Astrology was dismissed as superstition, and hemp was criminalized—largely due to political agendas and the rise of synthetic alternatives. The sacred became suspect. The natural was replaced with the synthetic.

In separating spirit from science and banning access to ancient wisdom, humanity experienced a disconnection—from the cosmos, from the earth, and from inner truth.

◈ A Renaissance of Remembering

Today, we're witnessing a profound reawakening. Astrology is no longer confined to horoscopes in magazines—it's used in psychological frameworks, coaching, and even corporate strategy. Birth charts are being explored for emotional insight, compatibility, and soul purpose.

Simultaneously, hemp—especially in its non-psychoactive form, CBD—is now legally accessible in much of the world. It's being studied and used for anxiety, inflammation, sleep, chronic pain, and neurological balance. Scientists are confirming what ancient medicine men and women already knew: this plant holds healing potential on multiple levels.

This modern renaissance isn't a coincidence—it's a cosmic correction. As global systems shift, people are craving connection, meaning, and natural solutions. The return to astrology and hemp is a return to wholeness.

◈ Why This Union Matters Now

We live in a time of overstimulation, anxiety, and uncertainty. Our systems—internal and societal—are taxed. Many are searching for healing that is deeper than symptom management. They want ritual. Rhythm. Empowerment. And authenticity.

Astrology provides a lens for understanding what's happening in your life and why. Hemp offers a grounded way to respond to those energies—calmly, consciously, and embodied. One offers the map. The other, the medicine.

When combined intentionally, astrology and hemp:

- Empower personal decision-making and timing.
- Help regulate mood, energy, and nervous system states.
- Provide a spiritual and sensory experience that reconnects you to cycles of nature and self.
- Create rituals that are uniquely tailored to your birth chart, your current transits, and your wellness needs.

◈ In Summary: The Reconnection Begins

Astrology and hemp are not trends. They are ancient technologies—sacred tools that helped our ancestors survive, thrive, and evolve. In a world spinning faster by the day, their return is an invitation to slow down, remember, and reconnect.

As we move forward in this book, we will dive into the zodiac signs, planetary influences, moon phases, solar shifts, and retrogrades—each paired with practical hemp recommendations and rituals to help you align with cosmic energies.

This is more than a wellness guide. It is a remembrance.

A return to rhythm.

A reconnection to the heavens and the healing plants beneath our feet.

Let the journey begin.

Chapter 2: Astrological Foundations for Beginners

Before we can align hemp with the cosmos, we must first understand the cosmic language itself. Astrology is not just about "what's your sign?"—it's a vast symbolic system rooted in mathematics, myth, observation, and energetics. It offers a map of the psyche, the body, and the soul, using the sky as its compass.

This chapter will serve as your beginner's guide to astrology, breaking down the essential components—signs, planets, elements, modalities, houses, and aspects—so you can start identifying how celestial forces uniquely shape your personality, mood, wellness, and response to the world.

◈ 1. The Zodiac Signs: The 12 Archetypes of Experience

The zodiac is a 360-degree wheel divided into 12 equal segments—each representing a **sign** with distinct characteristics, temperaments, and evolutionary lessons.

Sign	Element	Modality	Keywords	Ruling Planet
Aries	Fire	Cardinal	Bold, energetic, initiator	Mars
Taurus	Earth	Fixed	Grounded, sensual, loyal	Venus
Gemini	Air	Mutable	Curious, talkative, adaptable	Mercury

Sign	Element	Modality	Keywords	Ruling Planet
Cancer	Water	Cardinal	Nurturing, intuitive, emotionally deep	Moon
Leo	Fire	Fixed	Creative, proud, expressive	Sun
Virgo	Earth	Mutable	Precise, analytical, service-oriented	Mercury
Libra	Air	Cardinal	Harmonious, diplomatic, beauty-loving	Venus
Scorpio	Water	Fixed	Intense, transformative, mysterious	Pluto (Mars trad.)
Sagittarius	Fire	Mutable	Adventurous, optimistic, philosophical	Jupiter

Sign	Element	Modality	Keywords	Ruling Planet
Capricorn	Earth	Cardinal	Ambitious, structured, disciplined	Saturn
Aquarius	Air	Fixed	Visionary, rebellious, community-driven	Uranus (Sat. trad.)
Pisces	Water	Mutable	Empathic, dreamy, spiritual	Neptune (Jup. trad.)

Each zodiac sign represents a **unique energetic frequency**, not just a personality trait. For example, Cancer isn't just "emotional"—it's the archetype of the divine nurturer, teaching us how to feel, care, and protect.

In this book, we'll explore how each sign pairs with specific hemp qualities to support balance, health, and self-empowerment.

◈ 2. Planetary Rulers: The Influencers of the Sky

In astrology, **planets are the active forces**—the "verbs" of your birth chart. Each one governs specific themes in life and "rules" one or more zodiac signs, enhancing or expressing its energy.

Planet	Symbolizes	Rules
Sun	Core identity, vitality, life force	Leo
Moon	Emotions, intuition, inner world	Cancer
Mercury	Communication, thought, perception	Gemini, Virgo
Venus	Love, pleasure, aesthetics, values	Taurus, Libra
Mars	Action, drive, aggression, desire	Aries, (Scorpio tradition.)
Jupiter	Expansion, luck, belief, learning	Sagittarius, (Pisces trad.)
Saturn	Discipline, time, boundaries, mastery	Capricorn, (Aquarius trad.)
Uranus	Change, innovation, rebellion	Aquarius
Neptune	Dreams, illusion, spirituality, healing	Pisces

Planet	Symbolizes	Rules
Pluto	Transformation, power, death, rebirth	Scorpio

The planets are **always moving**, influencing not just your birth chart but your present experience through **transits** (temporary placements that affect mood, behavior, and energy).

◈ 3. The Four Elements: Your Energy Source

Each zodiac sign belongs to one of **four elemental families**. These describe how energy is experienced and expressed.

- **Fire (Aries, Leo, Sagittarius)**
  ◈ Enthusiastic, bold, instinctive, action-oriented
  Best hemp pairings: Sativa-dominant strains to complement focus, or CBD to temper impulsiveness.
- **Earth (Taurus, Virgo, Capricorn)**
  ◈ Practical, grounded, reliable, sensual
  Best hemp pairings: Topicals and edibles for physical healing and nourishment.
- **Air (Gemini, Libra, Aquarius)**
  ◈ Mental, communicative, analytical, social
  Best hemp pairings: Light vapes or hybrids for clarity and conversation.
- **Water (Cancer, Scorpio, Pisces)**
  ◈ Emotional, intuitive, imaginative, private
  Best hemp pairings: Indica strains, bath soaks, or tinctures for emotional balance.

Knowing your elemental profile helps guide your daily rituals, communication style, and even how you handle stress or sensory overload.

◈ **4. The Three Modalities: Movement and Momentum**

Each element is expressed in three different **modalities**—ways of operating or initiating action.

- **Cardinal Signs (Aries, Cancer, Libra, Capricorn)**
  Initiators, leaders, idea starters. Often benefit from hemp to ground overstimulation.
- **Fixed Signs (Taurus, Leo, Scorpio, Aquarius)**
  Stabilizers, builders, loyalists. Often need hemp for flexibility and release.
- **Mutable Signs (Gemini, Virgo, Sagittarius, Pisces)**
  Adapters, fluid thinkers, integrators. Often use hemp to anchor energy or improve focus.

Together, your **element + modality** shape your approach to change, healing, and ritual.

◈ 5. The Twelve Houses: Areas of Life Expression

In astrology, the **birth chart** is a circular map divided into 12 **houses**, each representing a domain of life. These "stages" show **where** planetary energies express themselves.

House	Theme	Keywords
1st	Self & identity	Personality, appearance, vitality
2nd	Values & possessions	Money, self-worth, material security
3rd	Communication & learning	Siblings, thought, expression
4th	Home & roots	Family, ancestry, emotional safety
5th	Creativity & pleasure	Romance, art, children, joy
6th	Health & service	Daily habits, body, organization
7th	Relationships & contracts	Marriage, partnerships, reflection
8th	Transformation & intimacy	Death, sex, rebirth, shared resources
9th	Belief & expansion	Philosophy, travel, spiritual learning
10th	Career & public image	Reputation, goals, status

House	Theme	Keywords
11th	Community & vision	Friendships, social causes, innovation
12th	Spirituality & subconscious	Dreams, karma, isolation, mysticism

As we progress through the book, you'll learn how hemp can support each house—like calming nerves in the 6th house of health, or aiding dreamwork in the mystical 12th.

◈ 6. Aspects: How Planets Relate to Each Other

Aspects are the angles formed between planets in your chart, revealing harmony or tension between internal forces.

Aspect	Angle	Description
Conjunction	0°	Two planets merge their energies
Sextile	60°	Easy flow, opportunity
Square	90°	Tension or challenge
Trine	120°	Natural ease and harmony
Opposition	180°	Polarized forces seeking integration

For example, a square between Mars and Neptune may create confusion in action or energy. Using hemp during such times can aid clarity, reflection, or calm during high-stress decisions.

◈ Pulling It All Together: A Personalized Cosmic Lens

Astrology is not deterministic—it is **descriptive**. It reveals patterns, potentials, and pathways to embodiment and evolution. When combined with hemp, astrology becomes not just insight, but **integration**. You can shift your moods, support your health, and navigate planetary shifts with natural, intentional tools.

Quick Example:

Let's say your Sun is in Leo (creative fire), your Moon is in Pisces (emotional water), and your Rising is Capricorn (structured earth). You might benefit from:

- A hemp-infused creative routine to energize your Leo expression
- Indica oils for calming Pisces's emotional sensitivity
- Structured CBD rituals to support Capricorn's need for control and predictability

This is the power of alignment—where knowledge of the stars meets grounded, natural practice.

Chapter 3: Hemp 101 — The Earth's Healer

Hemp is more than a plant—it is a symbol of resilience, utility, and holistic healing. As one of the first crops cultivated by humans, hemp has served ancient civilizations as food, fiber, medicine, and sacred tool. Today, it re-emerges as a keystone of the wellness movement, bridging the worlds of science and spirituality.

In this chapter, we demystify hemp by exploring its biological makeup, therapeutic compounds, ecological impact, and spiritual legacy. Whether you're new to hemp or seeking a deeper understanding, this chapter provides the foundational knowledge to support intentional use—especially when combined with astrological insight.

◈ **1. What Is Hemp? A Botanical Overview**

Hemp is a variety of the *Cannabis sativa* plant species. Unlike marijuana (also cannabis), hemp is bred to contain **low levels of THC (tetrahydrocannabinol)**—the psychoactive compound that causes a "high." By U.S. federal law, hemp must contain **0.3% THC or less**, making it non-intoxicating and legally distinct.

Key Parts of the Plant:

- **Seeds** – Rich in protein, omega-3s, and minerals. Used in nutrition and body care products.
- **Stalks** – Contain strong fibers ideal for textiles, rope, paper, and building materials.
- **Leaves and Flowers** – Contain cannabinoids and terpenes used for wellness and therapeutic products.

Hemp is not a drug. It is a **multi-purpose healing crop**—nutritive, medicinal, and ritualistic.

◈ 2. Cannabinoids: The Plant's Healing Compounds

Cannabinoids are chemical messengers unique to the cannabis plant. They interact with the **endocannabinoid system (ECS)**—a regulatory system in the human body that helps maintain balance in mood, immune function, sleep, pain, and more.

◈ Major Cannabinoids Found in Hemp:

- **CBD (Cannabidiol)**
  - Non-intoxicating
  - Anti-inflammatory, anxiolytic, neuroprotective
  - Balances emotional states, supports sleep, eases chronic pain
- **CBG (Cannabigerol)**
  - Known as the "mother cannabinoid"
  - Potential antimicrobial and mood-lifting effects
  - Emerging research suggests benefits for focus and clarity
- **CBN (Cannabinol)**
  - Mildly sedating
  - Often used for sleep and relaxation
- **Trace THC (<0.3%)**
  - Present in small amounts
  - May contribute to an "entourage effect" when combined with CBD

The **entourage effect** refers to how cannabinoids and terpenes work synergistically for greater healing potential than any single compound alone.

◈ 3. Terpenes: Nature's Aromatherapy

Terpenes are aromatic compounds found in many plants, but especially in hemp. They not only contribute to scent and flavor but also shape how a strain feels—relaxing, uplifting, focusing, or sedating.

◈ Common Terpenes in Hemp and Their Effects:

Terpene	Scent Profile	Potential Benefits
Limonene	Citrus, lemon	Uplifting, anti-anxiety, immune support
Myrcene	Earthy, musky	Sedative, anti-inflammatory, muscle relaxant
Pinene	Pine, forest	Alertness, memory aid, respiratory health
Linalool	Floral, lavender	Calming, anti-anxiety, anti-depressive
Caryophyllene	Peppery, spicy	Anti-inflammatory, pain relief, stress-reducing

Just as astrology aligns us with seasonal and cosmic energies, terpenes can help us choose hemp products that match the energetic tone we seek—stimulating during Aries season, calming during Pisces moon phases, etc.

◈ 4. The Legal Evolution of Hemp

Hemp has undergone a remarkable journey—revered, banned, and now reclaimed.

- **Ancient Use**: Cultivated for over 10,000 years across Asia, the Middle East, Africa, and Europe.
- **Colonial America**: Used for paper, clothing, rope, and even mandated by law for farmers in some colonies.
- **20th Century Ban**: Criminalized alongside marijuana during 1930s prohibition campaigns—despite no psychoactive effects.
- **Modern Renaissance**:
    - **2014 Farm Bill**: Allowed limited hemp cultivation for research.
    - **2018 Farm Bill**: Fully legalized industrial hemp production in the U.S.

Today, hemp is legal in many countries and regulated for THC content. Always check local laws when traveling or purchasing internationally.

◈ 5. Environmental Benefits: Hemp as Earth's Ally

Hemp is more than sustainable—it's **regenerative**. Unlike many crops that deplete the soil, hemp improves it.

◈ Eco-Advantages of Hemp:

- **Low water requirements**
- **Naturally pest-resistant**
- **Carbon-sequestering** – absorbs more CO_2 than most crops
- **Rapid growth cycle** – ready to harvest in 90–120 days
- **Phytoremediation** – cleans toxins from polluted soil

Hemp offers a powerful antidote to modern agricultural destruction. In the context of astrology, it symbolizes Virgo's purity, Capricorn's resourcefulness, and Aquarius's innovation—making it the plant of our planetary future.

◈ 6. Hemp as a Spiritual and Energetic Ally

For millennia, hemp has been used in spiritual rituals. In India, it was sacred to Shiva. In Tibet, it was consumed by monks for deep meditation. Across African and indigenous traditions, it was burned or brewed in ceremonies for connection to ancestors, intuition, and higher realms.

Hemp affects not just the physical body but also the **subtle energy field**, including:

- **Calming overactive thoughts** (beneficial for air signs)
- **Grounding during cosmic transits** (useful for fire or mutable-dominant charts)
- **Supporting nervous system repair during eclipses, retrogrades, or emotional upheaval**
- **Facilitating meditation, dreamwork, and journaling aligned with lunar cycles**

This makes hemp an ideal partner for **ritual, introspection, manifestation**, and **healing work** during major planetary alignments.

◈ 7. Selecting Hemp Products: A Quick Start

Not all hemp products are created equal. Here's a basic guide for newcomers:

Product Type	Best For	Example Use
CBD Oil/Tinctures	Full-body wellness, stress relief	Under tongue or in drinks daily
Topicals	Localized pain, skincare	Apply to sore muscles or inflammation
Capsules	Discreet, controlled dosing	Sleep support or anti-anxiety regimen
Edibles	Tasty and long-lasting effects	Use for prolonged relief or relaxation
Flower (smoke/vape)	Immediate relief, ritualistic use	Ideal for pre-meditation or journaling

In later chapters, we'll match specific product types to **zodiac traits, moon phases, retrogrades**, and **solar seasons** to help you craft your own cosmic wellness rituals.

◈ In Summary: Grounding the Cosmos

Hemp is more than a healing plant—it is an intelligent, adaptable, sacred ally. It brings clarity to the mind, calm to the heart, and restoration to the body. In a time when the world spins fast and chaos feels constant, hemp helps us slow down, breathe, and reconnect—with the earth, with the stars, and with ourselves.

By understanding the **botany, chemistry, history**, and **energetic nature** of hemp, we empower ourselves to use it consciously—not just for healing, but for transformation.

Chapter 4: Fire Signs — Igniting Purpose with Hemp

Aries, Leo, and Sagittarius explored through the lens of activation and motivation.

Fire signs are the cosmic catalysts of the zodiac. Ruled by passion, purpose, and bold expression, Aries, Leo, and Sagittarius radiate vitality and a drive for action. They're initiators, motivators, and trailblazers—each in their own way—but this elemental brilliance can also burn too hot without proper grounding, rest, or emotional regulation.

In this chapter, we explore the dynamic energy of fire signs and how hemp can enhance, stabilize, and channel their powerful frequencies into inspired leadership, creative radiance, and meaningful movement.

◈ The Fire Element: Essence and Expression

The fire signs share a desire to **inspire**, **create**, and **lead**. Their energy is outward-facing, proactive, and deeply intuitive—often acting on impulse or instinct. When balanced, they shine with charisma, confidence, and courage. When imbalanced, they may struggle with anger, burnout, restlessness, or egotism.

Sign	Modality	Ruling Planet	Core Themes
Aries	Cardinal	Mars	Initiative, bold action, personal courage
Leo	Fixed	Sun	Self-expression, confidence, creative power
Sagittarius	Mutable	Jupiter	Exploration, wisdom, optimism, expansion

Fire signs need hemp not to dim their flame—but to **direct it with purpose**, **sustain it over time**, and **temper it with wisdom**.

◈ Aries: The Initiator — Fueling Focused Action

Aries is the first sign of the zodiac, a pure surge of new beginnings and courageous momentum. Ruled by Mars, Aries often acts first and reflects later. Their boldness is admirable, but they can experience impulsiveness, restlessness, and frustration when blocked.

How Hemp Supports Aries:

- **CBD for Emotional Regulation**: Helps temper impulsive reactions and supports emotional clarity during conflict or decision-making.
- **Sativa-Dominant Strains**: Enhance Aries's drive while maintaining mental focus and creativity—perfect for launching new projects or leading bold initiatives.
- **Myrcene + Pinene Terpenes**: These compounds can support alertness, reduce inflammation from stress-based tension, and calm the nervous system after physical exertion.

Ritual Tip for Aries:

Use a CBD-infused tincture or roll-on before a competitive event, meeting, or workout. Pair with an intention-setting ritual during the waxing moon to supercharge your goal with grounded fire.

◈ Leo: The Performer — Radiating Creative Power

Leo, ruled by the Sun, is the heart-centered leader of the zodiac. They crave expression, recognition, and joy—and when aligned, they uplift everyone around them. However, their solar energy can burn too bright, leading to ego fatigue, performance anxiety, or emotional volatility.

How Hemp Supports Leo:

- **Balanced CBD:THC Blends**: Helps Leo harness creativity and confidence without tipping into overdrive or self-judgment.
- **Limonene and Linalool Terpenes**: Elevate mood, reduce self-doubt, and help Leos stay emotionally attuned while expressing themselves.
- **Topical CBD for Self-Care**: Leos thrive on pampering. Hemp-infused bath bombs, skin care products, or massage oils can enhance their glow inside and out.

Ritual Tip for Leo:

Create a self-love ritual on a Sunday (Leo's solar day) using hemp-infused candles and a mirror affirmation practice. Smoke a creativity-enhancing sativa while journaling your next artistic or personal milestone.

⬦ Sagittarius: The Seeker — Expanding with Intention

Sagittarius, ruled by expansive Jupiter, is the adventurer of the zodiac—craving truth, exploration, and philosophical insight. They're natural optimists but may struggle with commitment, distraction, or burnout from constant movement.

How Hemp Supports Sagittarius:

- **Sativa or Sativa-Leaning Hybrids**: Enhance mental clarity and creativity for writing, travel, or teaching. Keeps Sag grounded while still energized.
- **Pinene + Caryophyllene Terpenes**: Aid memory, support mental exploration, and reduce inflammation from physical or emotional overextension.
- **CBD Microdosing**: Supports consistency in rituals or long-term goals—a challenge for Sagittarians.

Ritual Tip for Sagittarius:

Try a "vision journaling" session during a full moon. Microdose with hemp tea or gummies, then write freely about your wildest dreams, next travel destination, or philosophical pursuit.

◈ Fire Sign Challenges & Hemp Solutions

Fire Sign Challenge	Suggested Hemp Strategy	Product Ideas
Burnout from overexertion	CBD isolate or topical hemp for recovery	Muscle balm, post-workout tincture
Emotional intensity	Linalool-dominant blends for mood balancing	Calming vape or oil blend
Impulsiveness or agitation	Full-spectrum CBD with myrcene + limonene	Gummies, capsule microdoses
Lack of patience	Ritual-based CBD use for slow, focused practice	Morning breathwork with CBD tea

◈◈ Fire + Hemp Rituals: Ignition With Intention

Fire signs benefit from rituals that keep their flame lit *with direction*. Hemp helps channel their enthusiasm into sustainable practices that fuel purpose, not chaos.

◈ Daily Practices:

- **Aries**: Hemp pre-workout + power affirmation ("I am fearless and focused.")
- **Leo**: Hemp-infused skincare + creativity meditation
- **Sagittarius**: Hemp journaling or reading ritual aligned with planetary transits

◈ Lunar Practices:

- **New Moon**: Set bold intentions with a hemp smoking ceremony
- **Full Moon**: Reflect on creative wins or emotional expansion with infused baths

◈ Elemental Enhancers:

- Use **candles, fire bowls, or incense** to accompany hemp rituals
- Work in the **Sun's light** for manifestation energy
- Pair hemp with **citrine, carnelian, or tiger's eye** for extra solar boost

◈ In Summary: Fanning the Flame, Not Burning Out

Fire signs are the zodiac's spark—without them, nothing begins. But even a wildfire needs control, focus, and fuel that lasts. Hemp becomes a sacred tool for refining their brilliance: calming overdrive, enhancing creativity, and anchoring purpose.

When Aries channels energy with intention, Leo expresses from the heart, and Sagittarius expands with wisdom—the fire element becomes not just action, but transformation.

Chapter 5: Earth Signs — Grounding in Ritual and Restoration

Taurus, Virgo, and Capricorn benefit from hemp through calming, detoxifying, and structural support.

Earth signs are the stabilizers, builders, and nurturers of the zodiac. Where fire signs inspire and initiate, earth signs manifest, refine, and sustain. They represent the element of form—what can be touched, built, and depended upon. Taurus, Virgo, and Capricorn each embody a unique dimension of grounded living: sensuality, purity, and structure.

This chapter explores how hemp synergizes with earth sign energy, offering calming routines, detoxifying support, and enhanced resilience. Through hemp, earth signs can deepen their rituals, preserve their health, and pursue real-world results with greater ease and flow.

◈ The Earth Element: Essence and Wisdom

The earth element is characterized by **stability**, **patience**, and **sensory intelligence**. Earth signs thrive in consistency, appreciate quality over speed, and are highly attuned to the physical body and material world. They find meaning in tangible success, sensory experience, and a well-tended routine.

Sign	Modality	Ruling Planet	Core Themes
Taurus	Fixed	Venus	Comfort, beauty, sensuality, slow growth
Virgo	Mutable	Mercury	Health, order, service, purification
Capricorn	Cardinal	Saturn	Discipline, ambition, structure, responsibility

Earth signs are **ritualistic by nature**, and hemp serves as the perfect ally in enhancing routines, supporting physical health, and grounding spiritual practice.

◈ Taurus: The Sensualist — Cultivating Comfort and Stillness

Taurus represents the garden of the zodiac. Governed by Venus, it seeks harmony through sensory pleasure, physical security, and the cultivation of inner peace. Slow and steady, Taurus resists chaos and thrives in environments that offer beauty, stability, and nourishment.

How Hemp Supports Taurus:

- **CBD-Infused Edibles and Teas**: Ideal for integrating into relaxing meals or nightly wind-downs.
- **Topical Hemp Skincare and Bath Rituals**: Taurus values self-pampering. Hemp lotions, oils, and bath soaks enhance both skin health and emotional calm.
- **Linalool + Myrcene Terpenes**: These promote deep relaxation, muscle relief, and emotional ease—perfect for Taurus's love of comfort.

Ritual Tip for Taurus:

Create a sensory sanctuary with hemp bath bombs, candlelight, and soft music. Perform this ritual on Fridays (Venus's day) for maximal heart-body harmony.

⬥ Virgo: The Purifier — Optimizing Wellness Through Precision

Virgo, ruled by Mercury, is the analyst and healer of the zodiac. This mutable earth sign is focused on improvement—of systems, bodies, and routines. Virgos seek purity and function, which can sometimes lead to overthinking, tension, or perfectionism.

How Hemp Supports Virgo:

- **CBD Capsules or Tinctures**: Easy to dose, discreet, and ideal for routine-driven wellness plans.
- **Hemp Seeds for Nutrition**: Virgo thrives on clean eating. Hemp seeds are rich in omega-3s, protein, and fiber, supporting digestive and cellular health.
- **Pinene + Caryophyllene Terpenes**: Promote mental clarity and reduce inflammation caused by stress or overanalysis.

Ritual Tip for Virgo:
Add a CBD tincture to your herbal tea during your nightly wind-down. Pair with journaling or breathwork to clear your mental clutter and reconnect with the body.

⬦ **Capricorn: The Builder — Grounding Ambition Into Achievement**

Capricorn is the architect of the zodiac, ruled by Saturn. This cardinal earth sign values discipline, long-term goals, and self-mastery. Often shouldering great responsibility, Capricorns can experience chronic tension, overwork, and emotional suppression.

How Hemp Supports Capricorn:

- **Full-Spectrum CBD for Stress Relief**: Helps ease rigidity and support nervous system resilience during high-demand periods.
- **Hemp-Based Muscle Recovery Products**: Topical creams or roll-ons for sore joints and muscles after long work sessions.
- **Caryophyllene + Myrcene Terpenes**: These terpenes target inflammation, grounding the body while supporting emotional release.

Ritual Tip for Capricorn:

Design a weekly hemp ritual focused on physical recovery—such as a Sunday night bath, foam rolling, and deep breathing with hemp topicals. This ensures Capricorn's "engine" doesn't burn out.

◈ Earth Sign Challenges & Hemp Solutions

Earth Sign Challenge	Hemp Strategy	Recommended Product Types
Overworking or rigidity	Full-spectrum CBD for nervous system balance	Tinctures, capsules, or functional teas
Stress or digestive upset	Hemp seeds and edibles to soothe the gut	Hemp protein, smoothies, seed bars
Physical tension	Topicals with myrcene and caryophyllene	Creams, balms, bath soaks
Perfectionism or anxiety	CBD with calming terpenes for emotional grounding	Nightly vape, tincture, or calming gummy blend

◇◇ **Earth + Hemp Rituals: Rooted in Rhythms**

Earth signs thrive when they **ritualize consistency**—turning simple acts into sacred self-care. Hemp enhances these rituals by providing structure, balance, and physical renewal.

◇ **Daily Practices:**

- **Taurus**: Hemp tea at sunset + grounding yoga or music
- **Virgo**: Morning tincture + structured journaling or checklist routine
- **Capricorn**: Hemp capsule midday + time-blocking for rest + productivity

◇ **Lunar Practices:**

- **New Moon**: Plant hemp seeds or intentions—literal or symbolic—especially in Taurus or Virgo moons
- **Full Moon**: Use a body-cleansing hemp ritual to release tension and prepare for the next work cycle

◇ **Elemental Enhancers:**

- **Soil, stone, and sound**: Add crystals like green aventurine, smoky quartz, or moss agate during hemp rituals
- **Ritual objects**: Herbal bundles, clay, wood bowls, and written affirmations support tangible grounding
- **Seasonal timing**: Earth signs thrive in the waxing gibbous moon (build-up phase)

◈ In Summary: Hemp for Embodied Mastery

Earth signs are here to teach us how to build a life of **meaning, health, and security**. Through their connection to the material world, they remind us that consistency is spiritual, and slow is sacred. Hemp is a natural complement to their frequency—offering a return to the body, the breath, and the sacred routine.

With hemp as their ally, Taurus finds peace through the senses, Virgo purifies through structure, and Capricorn builds with resilience. These grounded souls become the foundation for wellness practices that **last**, **heal**, and **grow**.

Chapter 7: Water Signs — Emotional Healing and Inner Peace
Cancer, Scorpio, and Pisces turn to hemp for emotional grounding, spiritual insight, and introspective depth.

Water signs are the empaths, mystics, and emotional navigators of the zodiac. Guided not by logic or structure, but by **feeling, intuition**, and **subtle energy**, Cancer, Scorpio, and Pisces dive into the depths of the human experience. They are attuned to moods, memories, and mysteries—making them natural healers, artists, and protectors. Yet their sensitivity often leaves them vulnerable to overwhelm, energetic burnout, and emotional entanglement.

In this chapter, we explore how hemp harmonizes with water sign frequencies—soothing anxiety, deepening spiritual practices, and helping to transform emotional weight into clarity and power.

◈ The Water Element: Depth and Devotion

The water element is associated with the **emotional body**, **intuition**, and the **subconscious mind**. Water signs tend to absorb their environment like a sponge—taking on other people's emotions, holding generational memory, and often retreating into inner sanctums for safety.

Sign	Modality	Ruling Planet	Core Themes
Cancer	Cardinal	Moon	Nurturing, protection, home, emotional memory
Scorpio	Fixed	Pluto (trad. Mars)	Transformation, intensity, secrecy, soul-depth
Pisces	Mutable	Neptune (trad. Jupiter)	Compassion, dreams, mysticism, transcendence

Hemp offers water signs an energetic buffer—a soothing, safe shoreline where their deep emotions can settle and process. It enables clarity in chaos, introspection without overwhelm, and emotional sovereignty.

◈ Cancer: The Nurturer — Creating Emotional Safety

Cancer is ruled by the Moon, which governs tides, moods, and memories. Cancer's instinct is to protect—to care deeply, quietly, and sometimes self-sacrificially. When emotionally imbalanced, Cancer may become withdrawn, passive-aggressive, or overly sensitive to perceived rejection.

How Hemp Supports Cancer:

- **CBD-Infused Comfort Foods**: Help regulate emotions through nourishing self-care rituals.
- **Full-Spectrum Hemp Oils**: Offer calming nervous system support during periods of stress or emotional intensity.
- **Linalool + Myrcene Terpenes**: Reduce anxiety, support sleep, and foster comfort in the body.

Ritual Tip for Cancer:

Create a bedtime ritual with a warm hemp drink, journaling, and moon-gazing. Add lavender essential oil and myrcene-rich hemp flower to promote calm, safe emotional release.

◈ Scorpio: The Transformer — Processing Intensity with Grace

Scorpio, ruled by Pluto, is the alchemist of the zodiac. These fixed water signs are drawn to the unseen, unspoken, and unexplored. They thrive on depth—of connection, of knowledge, of emotion. But without balance, Scorpio may descend into obsessive thoughts, control struggles, or emotional walls.

How Hemp Supports Scorpio:

- **CBD + THC Microdosing**: Supports emotional regulation while preserving Scorpio's need for full-spectrum intensity.
- **Caryophyllene + Limonene Terpenes**: Support mood elevation and reduce stress from over-controlling tendencies or paranoia.
- **Hemp Journaling Rituals**: Aid in shadow work, grief processing, and truth-telling without emotional overload.

Ritual Tip for Scorpio:

Light a black candle, smoke a hemp pre-roll, and write out emotional truths that need release. Burn or bury the paper after as a symbolic act of transformation.

◈ Pisces: The Mystic — Soothing the Soul and Awakening Dreams

Pisces, ruled by Neptune, dissolves boundaries. These mutable water signs are deeply spiritual, imaginative, and often porous to others' energies. Pisces seeks unity with the divine, but this openness can lead to escapism, emotional confusion, or energetic depletion.

How Hemp Supports Pisces:

- **CBD-Infused Meditations**: Calm the nervous system and create a bridge between dream and waking life.
- **Limonene + Linalool Terpenes**: Elevate mood while easing the overwhelm of being "too open" energetically.
- **Hemp Oils for Ritual Baths**: Provide purification and energetic reset after emotional absorption or psychic overload.

Ritual Tip for Pisces:
Prepare a spiritual bath with hemp oil, epsom salt, sea shells, and soft music. Use this time to decompress, re-center, and invite divine messages through visualization.

◈ Water Sign Challenges & Hemp Solutions

Water Sign Challenge	Hemp Strategy	Recommended Products
Emotional Overwhelm	Full-spectrum CBD with linalool or myrcene	Teas, tinctures, or edibles
Absorbing others' emotions	Protective rituals with hemp before social events	Pre-rolls, bath soaks, hemp energy shields
Sleep disturbances	Hemp with myrcene, CBN, and calming terpenes	Bedtime gummies, nighttime tincture blends
Emotional stagnation	Hemp-enhanced shadow work and release rituals	Journaling kits, smoke blends, hemp ritual candles

◈◈ Water + Hemp Rituals: Intuition, Healing, and Flow

Water signs crave depth. Their rituals are sacred, soulful, and transformative. Hemp deepens their ability to feel without drowning, love without losing self, and intuit without overload.

◈ Daily Practices:

- **Cancer**: CBD-infused herbal tea during morning affirmations or caregiving routines
- **Scorpio**: Microdose during shadow work journaling or meditation
- **Pisces**: Use hemp aromatherapy while painting, composing music, or channeling visions

◈ Lunar Practices:

- **New Moon**: Intention-setting bath rituals with hemp oil and moonstone
- **Full Moon**: Emotional release practices with hemp journaling and fire ceremonies

◈ Elemental Enhancers:

- **Water bowls, seashells, glass jars, and blue/white candles** complement water rituals
- **Moonstone, amethyst, and aquamarine** enhance intuitive perception
- Perform rituals near natural water or with background soundscapes of ocean, rain, or streams

◈ In Summary: Emotional Sovereignty with Sacred Support

Water signs remind us of what it means to feel, to empathize, and to transform through emotion. Yet their great strength can become a burden without boundaries, clarity, and recovery. Hemp serves as their sacred anchor—helping them hold space for themselves with gentleness, intention, and spiritual grace.

Cancer finds safety in the body.
Scorpio transmutes pain into power.
Pisces dissolves illusion and receives divine flow.

Together, the water signs—grounded by hemp—reclaim their emotional wisdom without losing themselves in the tides.

Chapter 8: Hemp for the Sun, Moon, and Rising Signs

Go beyond the Sun sign. This chapter helps readers tailor hemp use to their full astrological blueprint—emotional (Moon), public persona (Rising), and core essence (Sun).

Astrology is often reduced to just the Sun sign—the one based on your birthday. While the Sun sign is foundational, it's only a **one-third glimpse into your inner architecture**. Your full expression of self includes the **Sun**, **Moon**, and **Rising** (or Ascendant) signs—each representing distinct dimensions of personality and purpose.

When integrating hemp into your wellness rituals, recognizing the unique influence of these three pillars allows for **highly personalized healing**, attunement, and empowerment. Hemp becomes more than a calming tool—it becomes a vehicle for self-alignment across mind, body, and soul.

◈ **The Sun Sign — Your Core Identity**

The Sun represents your **essence**, **will**, and **creative life force**. It governs your ego, motivation, and the deeper "why" behind your goals and choices. Working with hemp in alignment with your Sun sign enhances your **sense of vitality**, **authenticity**, and **purpose**.

◈ **How to Use Hemp for the Sun Sign:**

* Support your Sun's **energy style** (fire, earth, air, or water) through matching terpene profiles and product types.
* Use **daily hemp rituals** to empower your natural strengths or soothe tendencies toward burnout or ego-driven stress.
* Anchor your **solar purpose** through creative, consistent use of hemp (journaling, movement, self-expression).

Sun Element	Hemp Intention Example
Fire	Energize and focus without burnout
Earth	Ground and structure productivity
Air	Stimulate creativity with calm communication
Water	Protect emotional sensitivity while creating

◈ **Ritual Suggestion:** Each morning, pair your hemp use with a 5-minute solar intention-setting practice. Speak aloud one action your Sun sign would be proud of today.

◈ **The Moon Sign — Your Emotional Body**

The Moon governs your **inner world**, emotional needs, unconscious patterns, and instincts. It represents what makes you feel safe, nurtured, and whole—your private self. For many, the Moon sign reveals more about how you react to stress than the Sun does.

Hemp used in alignment with your Moon sign can **regulate your emotional nervous system**, provide grounding for triggers, and support **soothing rituals** that help you process life at a heart-deep level.

◈ **How to Use Hemp for the Moon Sign:**

- Choose **delivery methods** that reflect your Moon sign's coping mechanisms (soothing baths for water moons, oral tinctures for air moons).
- Use **terpenes and cannabinoids** that help soothe nervous responses (linalool for anxiety-prone moons, caryophyllene for deep-seated stress).
- Align your hemp use with **lunar cycles** for intuitive attunement and release.

Moon Element	Hemp Self-Care Style
Fire	Calm emotional reactivity with CBD and movement
Earth	Nourish with routine and grounding food rituals
Air	Journal thoughts + use aromatherapy for clarity
Water	Deep bath soaks, emotional ritual + dreamwork

◈ **Ritual Suggestion:** Use hemp-infused lotion before bed while meditating on what your Moon sign needs to feel emotionally secure.

◇ The Rising Sign — Your Aura and Interface

The Rising (or Ascendant) sign is the **mask you wear in public**, your **instinctive behavior**, and how others perceive you on first impression. It represents your body's energetic shield and the path you walk through life. In many ways, the Rising sign is the **portal through which your whole chart expresses itself**.

Hemp used in accordance with your Rising sign helps **strengthen your confidence**, manage **social stress**, and align with your unique aesthetic and presence. It also plays a key role in **ritual design**—choosing the tone, tools, and timing that feel naturally you.

◇ How to Use Hemp for the Rising Sign:

- Choose hemp products that reflect how you **like to feel physically and socially**.
- Use rituals that enhance your **sense of self in motion**—from style to posture to voice.
- Support your **immune and energetic boundary system** with hemp to protect your daily interactions.

Rising Element	Hemp Ritual Aesthetic
Fire	Assertive morning tinctures for confidence
Earth	Grounded movement paired with topicals
Air	Social preparation with hemp teas + clarity
Water	Protection rituals before public exposure

◈ **Ritual Suggestion:** Before entering any social or work event, apply a hemp-based scent, balm, or drop under the tongue aligned with your Rising sign's energy.

◈ **Building Your Custom Hemp Blueprint**

To harmonize all three core signs, you can create a **daily hemp blueprint** that meets you on multiple levels:

◈ **Example Blueprint:**

- **Morning (Sun sign focus)** — Energizing tincture + solar affirmation
- **Midday (Rising sign focus)** — Social shield or creative CBD microdose
- **Evening (Moon sign focus)** — Deep emotional ritual with hemp soak or edible

◈ **Pro Tip:** If your Sun, Moon, and Rising are in different elements (e.g., Fire Sun, Earth Moon, Air Rising), your body may need different **cannabinoid balances** or **multiple delivery formats** for harmony.

◈ **Navigating Conflict Between Sun, Moon, and Rising**

Sometimes your Sun, Moon, and Rising signs can feel like **different people**—a Leo Sun wanting to shine, a Cancer Moon needing quiet, and a Virgo Rising craving order. Hemp can help bridge these internal differences by:

- **Balancing overstimulation** when signs clash (e.g., Fire and Water)
- **Creating rituals for compromise** (e.g., journaling out a plan where all three signs get time to "speak")
- **Anchoring the body** while allowing the psyche to process conflicting desires

Use hemp to soften these internal tensions and allow all parts of you to show up with integrity.

◈ In Summary: The Full Self, Activated

Your Sun is your fire, your Moon your water, your Rising your wind. Together, they form the holy trinity of **personality, purpose, and perception**.

Hemp, when used with this full awareness, becomes more than a wellness supplement—it becomes a **ritual compass**. A healing ally. A bridge between body, mind, and soul.

- **Sun:** Empower your core.
- **Moon:** Soothe your soul.
- **Rising:** Express your presence.

When you honor all three, you move through the world as your whole self—rooted, radiant, and real.

Chapter 9: Lunar Cycles and Hemp Rituals

Harness the power of the moon. Align your hemp use with New Moon intentions, Full Moon release, and the waxing/waning cycle for emotional and spiritual alignment.

The Moon is more than a celestial light in the night sky—it is Earth's energetic metronome. Its phases govern tides, influence sleep and emotions, and mark powerful moments for renewal, growth, and release. Across cultures and centuries, humans have used lunar cycles for planting, birthing, divination, and ritual.

When we integrate **hemp** into lunar practices, we activate a unique synergy: the **calming, grounding energy of hemp** paired with the **rhythmic pull of the moon**. Together, they create a potent ritual framework that supports emotional healing, spiritual evolution, and energetic alignment.

This chapter explores how to pair specific hemp products and rituals with each lunar phase, guiding you to deepen your connection with both the **earth's medicine** and the **moon's wisdom**.

◈ New Moon — Planting Seeds with Intention

The New Moon is a time of **darkness and potential**. Symbolizing a fresh start, it is ideal for setting intentions, visualizing goals, and calling in what you desire. It's not a time for outward action, but for inward alignment.

Energetic Themes:

- Initiation
- Vision
- Seeding potential
- Rest and reset

Hemp Integration:

- Use **CBD-rich tinctures or teas** to calm the nervous system and encourage clarity in goal setting.
- Choose **linalool or pinene terpenes** to promote clear visualization and emotional calm.

New Moon Ritual:

1. Find a quiet, dark space with no distractions.
2. Use a **hemp-infused tea** or dropper while journaling 3–5 intentions you wish to cultivate.
3. Burn a white or silver candle.
4. Speak your intentions aloud, then close your eyes and visualize your future self already embodying them.
5. Seal the ritual with breathwork or gentle stretching.

◇ *Astrological Tip:* The zodiac sign the New Moon occurs in will flavor your intention. A New Moon in Virgo? Focus on routines and health. In Sagittarius? Focus on travel and learning.

◈ **Waxing Moon — Building Momentum and Structure**

From the New Moon to the Full Moon, the waxing phase symbolizes **growth, expansion, and development**. It's a great time to take action, research, and build the foundation for your goals.

Energetic Themes:

- Growth
- Motivation
- Structure and strategy
- Attracting supportive energies

Hemp Integration:

- Choose **energizing CBD blends or balanced hybrid strains** to support productivity and follow-through.
- Terpenes like **limonene and beta-caryophyllene** help uplift mood and strengthen mental focus.

Waxing Moon Ritual:

1. Create a "ritual workspace" with a **hemp-infused roll-on**, essential oils, and a vision board.
2. Each day, apply hemp topicals to your wrists or neck before beginning tasks aligned with your New Moon goals.
3. Incorporate **CBD capsules** for consistent, calm focus during this action-heavy phase.

◈ *Astrological Tip:* This is the best phase to start habit-building hemp routines—microdosing, journaling, or daily teas.

◈ Full Moon — Release, Realization, and Ritual

The Full Moon is a time of **illumination**, where energy peaks and emotions often surface. It can bring clarity, closure, and celebration—or chaos. It's a potent moment for reflection, release, and letting go of what no longer serves you.

Energetic Themes:

- Clarity
- Culmination
- Emotional intensity
- Release and forgiveness

Hemp Integration:

- Use **high-CBD or indica-dominant hemp** to manage emotional overwhelm and foster introspection.
- Terpenes like **myrcene and linalool** enhance the release of stress and trauma.

Full Moon Ritual:

1. Take a **hemp-infused bath** with salt, crystals, and herbs (e.g., lavender, mugwort).
2. Write down what you are ready to release—emotions, patterns, relationships.
3. Light a black or deep blue candle.
4. Burn the list in a fire-safe bowl and visualize the smoke releasing your burdens.
5. Follow with a calming **CBD edible** or tea to anchor the experience.

◈ *Astrological Tip:* The Full Moon sign will highlight which life area is being completed or illuminated. A Full Moon in Taurus? Focus on finances and stability. In Pisces? Focus on spiritual or emotional closure.

◈ **Waning Moon — Integration, Detox, and Rest**

The waning phase (after the Full Moon until the New Moon) is a time of **surrender, stillness, and preparation**. It's perfect for rest, cleansing, and tying up loose ends before beginning anew.

Energetic Themes:

- Decluttering
- Spiritual retreat
- Recovery
- Preparation for rebirth

Hemp Integration:

- Use **hemp topicals and slow-release formats** like edibles for restoration and sleep.
- Pair with **CBN and myrcene**-rich products to support deep relaxation and dream work.

Waning Moon Ritual:

1. Perform a gentle body scan with hemp salve or lotion, massaging areas of tension.
2. Use this time for **digital detox**, unplugging from external noise.
3. Journal your emotional state and any signs or dreams that arose during the Full Moon.
4. Use a calming **CBD diffuser** or hemp oil during meditation to promote inner stillness.

◈ *Astrological Tip:* This is a time for spiritual maintenance—use hemp to support shadow work, emotional release, and physical detox.

◈ Creating a Monthly Hemp + Moon Calendar

Lunar Phase	Focus	Hemp Ritual Type
New Moon	Set intentions	Journaling + CBD tea
Waxing Moon	Build structure and take action	Microdosing + vision board
Full Moon	Release and reflect	Bath rituals + high-CBD edibles
Waning Moon	Rest and integrate	Topicals + dreamwork tinctures

Consider syncing your **hemp product selection**, terpene blends, and ritual format to the lunar calendar monthly. This creates a cycle of wellness that mirrors the **ebb and flow of nature**, deepening your awareness and embodiment.

◈ In Summary: Sacred Cycles in Synergy

The Moon is a sacred mirror—reflecting not just light, but emotional truth, timing, and transformation. Hemp is the Earth's gentle medicine—offering clarity, calm, and support as we move through each lunar doorway.

When paired together, they offer a **ritual rhythm** that grounds your wellness practices, supports your inner evolution, and aligns you with the very fabric of nature itself.

Let your emotions flow like tides, and let hemp be your anchor in every phase.

Chapter 10: Solar Seasons and Hemp Wellness

Celebrate the solstices and equinoxes with seasonal hemp rituals. Each zodiac season (Aries to Pisces) offers unique energy for cultivating physical and energetic renewal.

As the Earth orbits the Sun, it passes through the twelve zodiac signs, marking **distinct solar seasons** that influence collective energy, weather, mood, and biological rhythms. These zodiac seasons align with the **solstices**, **equinoxes**, and **quarter turns** of nature's wheel. Each carries a unique vibration, inviting us to recalibrate our wellness practices, set new priorities, and reconnect with life's cyclical flow.

When we incorporate **hemp into solar season rituals**, we bring **bodily support to seasonal shifts**, balancing both inner and outer changes. Hemp becomes the sacred plant that travels with us through the year—grounding fire, hydrating dryness, warming cold, and cooling heat.

In this chapter, you'll learn how to design **seasonal hemp rituals** based on each zodiac sign's solar phase, helping you live in alignment with the natural world and optimize physical, emotional, and spiritual vitality year-round.

⬧ **Spring Equinox — Initiation & Growth (Aries, Taurus, Gemini)**

March 20–June 20

The Spring Equinox is a threshold of **balance and rebirth**. Light and dark are equal, and nature awakens with new energy. It is a time of renewal, intention-setting, and outward action.

⬧ **Aries Season (March 21–April 19)**

- **Vibe**: Action, courage, beginnings
- **Hemp Ritual**: Energizing sativa hemp blends with limonene or pinene
- **Practice**: Wake-and-rise tincture with solar affirmations
- **Goal**: Ignite motivation without burnout

⬧ **Taurus Season (April 20–May 20)**

- **Vibe**: Stability, sensuality, self-worth
- **Hemp Ritual**: Full-spectrum CBD for grounding + hemp-infused skincare
- **Practice**: Earth-touching barefoot walks, mindful eating with hemp oil
- **Goal**: Anchor abundance and inner peace

⬧ **Gemini Season (May 21–June 20)**

- **Vibe**: Curiosity, learning, communication
- **Hemp Ritual**: Balanced hybrids or hemp teas with limonene for clarity
- **Practice**: Hemp journaling, social rituals, expressive art
- **Goal**: Connect mind and speech

◈ Summer Solstice — Radiance & Expansion (Cancer, Leo, Virgo)

June 21–September 22

The longest day of the year. The Sun is at its peak, and so are vitality, playfulness, and expression. It's a time for nourishing joy, creating memories, and strengthening emotional bonds.

◈ Cancer Season (June 21–July 22)

- **Vibe**: Nurture, home, emotional intuition
- **Hemp Ritual**: CBD-rich bath soaks, comfort oils, and soft sleep tinctures
- **Practice**: Nightly tea with moon-gazing; dream journaling
- **Goal**: Emotional regulation and safety

◈ Leo Season (July 23–August 22)

- **Vibe**: Leadership, passion, creative joy
- **Hemp Ritual**: Uplifting hemp smoke blends or solar-infused oils
- **Practice**: Morning mirror rituals with hemp balm affirmations
- **Goal**: Embody boldness without ego overdrive

◈ Virgo Season (August 23–September 22)

- **Vibe**: Health, precision, service
- **Hemp Ritual**: Capsules or tinctures for digestion, hemp foot soaks
- **Practice**: Weekly body journaling with hemp aroma rituals
- **Goal**: Heal the vessel with discipline and love

⬦ Autumn Equinox — Harvest & Balance (Libra, Scorpio, Sagittarius)

September 23–December 20

As day and night balance again, we shift inward—harvesting our growth, refining our focus, and preparing for inner descent. It is a season of gratitude, transition, and reevaluation.

⬦ Libra Season (September 23–October 22)

- **Vibe**: Harmony, beauty, relationships
- **Hemp Ritual**: CBD topicals for touch, skin care, and shared relaxation
- **Practice**: Partnered tea ceremonies or shared smoking rituals
- **Goal**: Find relational ease and aesthetic balance

⬦ Scorpio Season (October 23–November 21)

- **Vibe**: Depth, truth, transformation
- **Hemp Ritual**: Shadow work with hemp-infused incense and journaling
- **Practice**: Full Moon release ritual with smoke + fire
- **Goal**: Transmute pain into power

⬦ Sagittarius Season (November 22–December 21)

- **Vibe**: Adventure, philosophy, freedom
- **Hemp Ritual**: Sativa-forward blends or energizing hemp snacks
- **Practice**: Movement rituals—yoga, walking meditations, forest hikes
- **Goal**: Expand joyfully with presence

◈ Winter Solstice — Reflection & Renewal (Capricorn, Aquarius, Pisces)

December 21–March 19

The darkest time of year. The Winter Solstice is a portal of **stillness, introspection, and spiritual renewal**. It invites rest, review, and deep-rooted transformation.

◈ Capricorn Season (December 22–January 19)

- **Vibe**: Mastery, structure, ambition
- **Hemp Ritual**: Consistent hemp supplement routines and planning rituals
- **Practice**: Goal-setting with CBD tea; sacred structure creation
- **Goal**: Build systems that support peace and productivity

◈ Aquarius Season (January 20–February 18)

- **Vibe**: Innovation, vision, collective change
- **Hemp Ritual**: Brain-boosting blends; hemp group meditations
- **Practice**: Vision boarding with cannabinoids + sound healing
- **Goal**: Rebel with purpose and clarity

◈ Pisces Season (February 19–March 20)

- **Vibe**: Dreaming, dissolving, spiritual surrender
- **Hemp Ritual**: Bedtime hemp oil blends with linalool and myrcene
- **Practice**: Intuitive bath rituals; channeled writing with hemp smoke
- **Goal**: Let go and return to source

◈ Creating Your Personal Hemp Solar Calendar

Sync your hemp use with each **solar shift** to support your energy, detox your mind, and reconnect with seasonal rhythms.

Season	Element	Focus	Suggested Hemp Ritual
Spring	Air/Earth	Initiation, growth	Energizing blends, vision boards
Summer	Fire/Water	Joy, connection, radiance	Creative hemp rituals, social gatherings
Autumn	Air/Water	Harvest, release, reflection	Shadow journaling, detox baths
Winter	Earth/Air	Restoration, vision, planning	Sleep support, visioning teas and stillness

◈ *Tip:* Combine your **Sun sign's season** with its opposite for balance. (Leo ↔ Aquarius, Taurus ↔ Scorpio)

◈ In Summary: The Year as Ritual

The journey from Aries to Pisces is a sacred loop—one that echoes the life cycle itself. Each solar season invites different needs, moods, and desires. With hemp as your botanical ally, you can flow with the Sun's journey, not against it.

◈ Aries begins the spark.

◈ Leo radiates the fire.

◈ Scorpio reveals the truth.

◈ Pisces dissolves into the void.

Let hemp guide your body through every solar shift, offering the grounding, vitality, and serenity needed to meet the moment fully.

Chapter 11: Planetary Retrogrades — Hemp for Reflection

Discover how to survive Mercury retrograde and other planetary retrogrades with the help of hemp. Includes therapeutic strategies for internal navigation and balance.

In astrology, **retrogrades** are periods when a planet appears to move backward in the sky from Earth's perspective. These cosmic events are not merely optical illusions—they are energetic invitations for **pause, review, and recalibration**. Every planet that goes retrograde influences a particular aspect of life: from communication and love to career, belief systems, and even the subconscious.

Unfortunately, retrogrades have a bad reputation. Mercury retrograde, in particular, is often blamed for tech failures, travel issues, and miscommunication. But the deeper purpose of retrogrades isn't chaos—it's **correction**. They offer a sacred space to **revisit what we've rushed, rethink what we've believed**, and **restructure what we've built**.

Hemp is an invaluable ally during these reflective cycles. With its anti-inflammatory, neuroregulatory, and emotionally grounding properties, hemp soothes the body while supporting the mental clarity needed to navigate these energetically reversed periods. In this chapter, we'll examine each planet's retrograde theme and how to pair it with **intentional hemp strategies** for therapeutic self-care and internal growth.

◈ Mercury Retrograde — Communication, Tech & Thought

Frequency: 3–4 times per year
Duration: ~3 weeks
Themes:

- Misunderstandings
- Delayed communication
- Revisions and reflection
- Mental overload or fog

Hemp Strategy:

- Use **CBD oils or tinctures** to manage overthinking and reduce mental tension.
- Incorporate **terpenes like pinene (clarity)** and **limonene (mood support)**.
- Try **CBD vapes or teas** before important conversations to calm reactive speech.

Ritual Tip: Journal your thoughts after each day to reduce mental buildup. Pair with a calming hemp tea and lavender essential oil.

⬧ **Venus Retrograde — Love, Beauty & Self-Worth**
Frequency: Every 18 months
Duration: ~6 weeks
Themes:

- Reassessment of relationships
- Revisiting past lovers or self-image
- Reevaluation of values and aesthetics

Hemp Strategy:

- Use **CBD-infused bath rituals** with rose or jasmine for heart chakra healing.
- Apply **hemp-based skincare** as a self-love ritual.
- Choose **linalool-heavy strains** for emotional soothing and introspection.

Ritual Tip: Create a mirror ritual where you apply hemp balm or lotion while affirming your evolving worth and beauty. Ask yourself, "What do I truly value now?"

◈ Mars Retrograde — Motivation, Anger & Action

Frequency: Every 2 years
Duration: ~2 months
Themes:

* Blocked ambition
* Frustration and irritability
* Repressed anger surfacing

Hemp Strategy:

* Use **high-CBD, low-THC blends** to temper aggressive emotional waves.
* Integrate **myrcene or caryophyllene** for physical tension and inflammation.
* Ground energy with **hemp oils in movement rituals** (e.g., yoga or tai chi).

Ritual Tip: Burn off stress with movement. Then unwind with a hemp soak or hemp massage balm for emotional release and physical reset.

◈ Jupiter Retrograde — Beliefs, Growth & Expansion

Frequency: Once per year
Duration: ~4 months
Themes:

- Spiritual detours
- Rethinking purpose or higher education
- Revisiting life philosophy

Hemp Strategy:

- Pair **hemp journaling with blue lotus or mugwort teas** to access spiritual insight.
- Use **limonene-forward blends** for vision work and optimism reset.
- Schedule **weekly solo rituals** to question and clarify your bigger why.

Ritual Tip: Create a "wisdom corner" with philosophical books, hemp incense, and a guided meditation playlist. Review your belief systems with a softened, open heart.

◈ Saturn Retrograde — Discipline, Karma & Boundaries

Frequency: Once per year
Duration: ~4–5 months
Themes:

- Life lessons resurfacing
- Revisiting commitments
- Authority, time, and self-discipline tests

Hemp Strategy:

- Incorporate **CBD gummies or capsules** for long-term stress support.
- Apply **structured hemp rituals** (same time each day) for grounding.
- Focus on **terpenes like caryophyllene and humulene** for structure and calm.

Ritual Tip: Write down every obligation that feels heavy. Use a hemp ritual to review and release what's no longer aligned. End with a sleep tincture and stillness.

◈ Uranus Retrograde — Innovation, Freedom & Disruption
Frequency: Once per year
Duration: ~5 months
Themes:

- Unexpected shifts in identity
- Sudden breakouts of creativity
- Internal rebellion or insight

Hemp Strategy:

- Choose **daytime clarity-enhancing hemp blends** with pinene for insight.
- Use **CBD topicals and breathwork** to help manage sudden anxiety.
- Support sleep during wild energetic shifts with myrcene-rich formulas.

Ritual Tip: During moments of chaos, ground with a CBD foot massage, then journal your rebellious ideas. What truth are you ready to express?

◈ **Neptune Retrograde — Illusion, Intuition & Escapism**
Frequency: Once per year
Duration: ~5–6 months
Themes:

- Heightened dreams or illusions
- Clarity about spiritual truths
- Increased sensitivity or escapism

Hemp Strategy:

- Use **CBN-heavy blends or myrcene/CBD combinations** for dreamwork.
- Incorporate **smoke rituals with lavender and hemp** to calm overstimulation.
- Avoid overuse of psychoactive substances—focus on **clarity and surrender**.

Ritual Tip: Keep a dream journal next to your hemp tea. Review what illusions are falling away and where truth is surfacing.

◈ Pluto Retrograde — Power, Shadow & Transformation

Frequency: Once per year
Duration: ~5–6 months
Themes:

- Shadow work and inner death
- Releasing old identities
- Facing control dynamics and rebirth

Hemp Strategy:

- Use **hemp + cacao ceremonies** to access the heart's hidden truths.
- Create deep **smoke cleansing rituals** with grounding hemp herbs.
- Pair with journaling and a soundtrack for inner confrontation and healing.

Ritual Tip: Meditate with a black candle, a hemp joint, and a question: *"What part of me is dying so something greater can be born?"*

◈ Navigating Retrogrades with a Ritual Map

Retrograde Planet	Focus Area	Hemp Ritual Type
Mercury	Mind/Tech	Journaling + tea + breathwork
Venus	Love/Self-worth	Skincare + bath + rose hemp oils
Mars	Anger/Drive	Movement + topical balms + stretching
Jupiter	Faith/Purpose	Tea + incense + vision journaling
Saturn	Responsibility	Routine rituals + CBD capsules
Uranus	Innovation	Foot soaks + idea journaling
Neptune	Dreams/Spirituality	Dream blends + sleep rituals
Pluto	Shadow/Power	Deep journaling + smoke ceremony

◈ In Summary: Rewind to Realign

Retrogrades aren't meant to halt your growth—they're meant to **reroute it**. These planetary cycles create sacred pauses for you to slow down, breathe deeper, and realign with your most authentic path. Hemp doesn't fix what's broken—but it offers the **energetic softness**, the **mental clarity**, and the **emotional spaciousness** to make meaning out of the rewind.

Let every retrograde become a retreat, not a regression. Let hemp be the earth's whisper guiding you through the stars' challenges—one breath, one cup, one ritual at a time.

Chapter 12: Astrological Gardening and Hemp Cultivation

A guide to biodynamic planting. Learn how to sow, tend, and harvest hemp using lunar phases, planetary aspects, and zodiacal guidance for a spiritually aligned yield.

In ancient times, agriculture was not merely practical—it was sacred. Farmers observed not only weather patterns but also the movements of the stars, the cycles of the moon, and the signs of the zodiac. **Astrological gardening**, also known as **biodynamic farming**, is the art of aligning your planting and harvesting with celestial timing to produce healthier, more energetically aligned crops.

As hemp makes its return to both wellness and spiritual communities, many growers are rediscovering how to **weave astrology into their cultivation practice**. Whether you grow hemp for ritual, self-care, or small-batch crafting, this chapter will guide you through the **celestial blueprint** of planting, growing, and harvesting your hemp crop with the cosmos as your partner.

◈ **The Lunar Planting Calendar**

The Moon governs moisture, tides, and the subtle flow of life force energy (chi or prana). Its cycle of approximately 29.5 days creates powerful energetic windows for various gardening tasks.

◈ **New Moon to First Quarter (Waxing Moon): Sowing & Germination**

- Energy is **building**.
- Plant seeds that grow **above ground**, like hemp.
- Ideal for initiating growth and rooting intention into soil.

◈ *Ritual Tip:* Place hemp seeds in your palm, bless them with your intention, and plant them during the **waxing crescent**. Water with moon-charged water.

◈ **Full Moon: Fertilization & Irrigation**

- Energy is at its **peak**.
- The gravitational pull draws water upward—plants are most **hydrated and receptive**.
- Ideal for fertilizing, pruning, and supporting growth.

◈ *Ritual Tip:* Add **hemp compost tea** or nutrient-rich water to your garden. Sit under the moonlight and visualize your plants absorbing moonlight and wisdom.

◇ **Last Quarter to New Moon (Waning Moon): Harvesting & Root Work**

- Energy is **receding**.
- Focus shifts below the surface—to **roots, bulbs, and inner strength**.
- Best for harvesting hemp flowers, trimming, and soil preparation.

◇ *Ritual Tip:* Harvest during the **waning gibbous** for strongest resin content. Say a gratitude prayer to the plant spirit before cutting.

◈ Zodiac Gardening Signs — Elemental Influence on Hemp

Each zodiac sign carries a unique elemental influence that affects plant vitality. When the Moon transits a sign, it temporarily imbues that energy into the Earth.

Element	Signs	Best For
◈ Earth	Taurus, Virgo, Capricorn	Root growth, structure, harvest
◈ Fire	Aries, Leo, Sagittarius	Flowering, fruiting, vitality
◈ Water	Cancer, Scorpio, Pisces	Leaf growth, emotional resonance
◈ Air	Gemini, Libra, Aquarius	Seed dispersal, pollination, drying

Example:

- **Moon in Taurus:** Excellent for planting hemp for body wellness and physical grounding.
- **Moon in Pisces:** Best for spiritual ritual blends or dream-enhancing hemp.
- **Moon in Leo:** Ideal for harvesting when vibrancy and solar potency are desired.

◈ Planetary Rulership and Hemp Vibration

Each planet influences plant growth in distinct ways. Understanding these influences allows you to choose the best days for specific cultivation tasks.

Planet	Governs	Gardening Tip
◈ Mercury	Movement, pollen, leaves	Use during airy signs for hemp tea or oils
♀ Venus	Fragrance, softness	Choose for nurturing hemp skincare strains
♂ Mars	Strength, roots	Best for pruning and tough stalks
◈ Jupiter	Expansion, abundance	Planting days for prosperity harvest
◈ Saturn	Structure, discipline	Focus on drying, curing, and soil prep
◈ Sun	Vitality, flowering	Use Leo days for harvesting resinous flowers
◈ Moon	Water, emotions	Use Cancer or Pisces days for ritual plants

◇ **Biodynamic Hemp Cultivation Practices**

To fully integrate astrology into your hemp garden, follow these principles:

1. Sowing by the Stars

- Use a lunar gardening calendar to time your sowing.
- Align with fertile signs (Cancer, Scorpio, Pisces, Taurus) for seed planting.
- Plant **early in the waxing moon** for energetic seedlings.

2. Tending with Intention

- Water during **Cancer or Pisces moons** to deepen emotional resonance.
- Prune during **Gemini or Virgo moons** to improve airflow and clarity.
- Use hemp mulch and compost charged under a Full Moon in Taurus for yield increase.

3. Harvesting Spiritually

- Harvest under **Capricorn** or **Scorpio** moons for grounding properties.
- Cut in the **waning moon** for stronger cannabinoid and terpene preservation.
- Use smoke or sound blessings (e.g., singing bowl, chimes) when cutting to honor the spirit of the plant.

4. Drying and Curing

- Dry your hemp when the Moon is in an **Air sign** (Gemini, Libra, Aquarius) for optimal airflow and energetic lightness.
- Cure slowly and in darkness to honor the retreating cycle of the Moon.

◈ Ritual: The Sacred Planting Ceremony

1. **Create a small altar near your garden** with your birth chart, hemp seeds, a candle, and a bowl of charged water.
2. On a **waxing crescent**, cleanse the seeds with the water while stating your intention (e.g., "May this plant grow in strength and sacred alignment").
3. Bury the seed, visualize it growing in harmony with the stars.
4. Light the candle as a symbol of solar vitality and place a moon-charged crystal in the soil nearby.
5. Offer gratitude and water regularly on Cancer moons.

◈ In Summary: Cultivating Celestial Harmony

Astrological gardening is not just about timing—it's about **tuning your spirit to the natural rhythm of creation**. Hemp is a sacred partner in this journey, thriving under cosmic care and responding to the wisdom of moon, planet, and zodiac.

By growing hemp in sync with the heavens, you're not just cultivating a plant—you're **nurturing intention, harvesting insight**, and **rooting your practice in the wisdom of the universe**.

Chapter 13: Crafting Personalized Hemp Rituals

Create intentional morning and evening routines aligned with your birth chart. Use CBD oils, edibles, or smoke rituals to energize, focus, or unwind.

Rituals are sacred acts of consistency, intention, and transformation. In the ancient world, every sunrise and sunset carried purpose—each a gateway to presence and renewal. When combined with **astrology** and the **healing properties of hemp**, these routines evolve into powerful personal tools for **energy alignment, mental clarity**, and **spiritual centering**.

This chapter offers a comprehensive framework for designing **personalized hemp rituals** based on your **natal chart**—with a focus on the **Sun, Moon, and Rising signs**, as well as elemental needs. Whether you prefer **CBD oils, edibles, hemp teas, or smoke rituals**, the goal is the same: to create supportive moments that match your **unique energy blueprint**, helping you start the day with presence and end it in peace.

◈ **Step 1: Know Thyself — Using Your Natal Chart as a Ritual Compass**

Your **birth chart** acts as your personal spiritual map. The following placements are essential to tailoring hemp rituals:

- ◈ **Sun Sign (Core Energy)** — Guides your vitality, purpose, and dominant energy patterns.
- ◈ **Moon Sign (Emotional Body)** — Reveals what comforts, soothes, or overwhelms you.
- ↗ **Rising Sign (Morning Mindset)** — Dictates your interface with the world and daily rhythm.
- ◈ **Elemental Balance** — Indicates which element you need more of in your life: grounding (Earth), flow (Water), passion (Fire), or breath (Air).

◈ *Example:* A Cancer Sun, Pisces Moon, and Virgo Rising individual may benefit from gentle, emotionally soothing morning rituals (Virgo + Water combo) and grounding herbal baths at night.

◈ **Morning Hemp Rituals — Rise in Alignment**

Morning is a portal of potential. Rather than jolting awake with stress, you can ease into your day with clarity, confidence, and energetic harmony.

◈ **Purpose:**

- Ground the nervous system
- Clarify intention
- Activate mental and physical vitality
- Connect to solar energy

◈ **Morning Ritual Elements:**

- **CBD Oil or Sublingual Tincture**: For stress-free alertness
- **Hemp Tea (with herbs like lemon balm or green tea)**: Light energy boost
- **Movement**: Gentle yoga, sun salutations, stretching
- **Breathwork + Affirmations**: Especially beneficial for Air and Fire signs
- **Journaling**: Align intention with planetary transits

◈ **Ritual by Element:**

Element	Morning Need	Hemp Support Example
Earth	Structure, calm	CBD capsules + grounding affirmations
Air	Focus, flexibility	Hemp tea + breath-focused journaling
Fire	Motivation, energy	Hemp-infused matcha or uplifting sativa blends
Water	Peace, softness	Hemp bath soaks or oil massage with soft music

◈ *Example Ritual for Leo Rising*:

- Morning sunlight exposure, CBD + citrus tea
- Mirror affirmations: "I radiate purpose and lead with heart"
- Five-minute dance or movement flow
- Focus meditation with a calendula and hemp balm on the heart center

◇ **Evening Hemp Rituals — Unwind and Realign**

Nighttime is when the mind digests the day, the body repairs itself, and the spirit calls for stillness. A well-crafted evening hemp ritual invites **restful sleep, emotional release,** and **spiritual re-centering.**

◇ **Purpose:**

- Detox the nervous system
- Process emotions
- Clear mental clutter
- Prepare for dreamwork or deep sleep

◇ **Evening Ritual Elements:**

- **CBD Oil or Edibles**: Deeper, longer-lasting calm
- **Smoke Rituals (lavender, mugwort, or myrcene-rich hemp)**: For releasing tension
- **Moon Journaling or Dream Tracking**: Especially for Water signs
- **Sacred Bath or Foot Soak**: Add Himalayan salt, dried herbs, and hemp oil
- **Sound Healing or Aromatherapy**: Pair hemp with calming frequencies

◈ **Ritual by Element:**

Element	Evening Need	Hemp Support Example
Earth	Detachment, stillness	Hemp topical massage + journaling
Air	Quieting the mind	Smoke ritual + guided breath meditation
Fire	Cooling passion	Indica blends with cooling peppermint oil
Water	Safe space, dreams	Hemp and lavender bath with dream journaling

◈ *Example Ritual for Pisces Moon*:

- Myrcene-heavy CBD edible 1 hour before bed
- Ritual bath with hemp oil, jasmine, and blue lotus
- Write a short gratitude list and dream intentions
- Sleep with calming music and a moon-charged crystal nearby

◈ Aligning with Planetary Transits and Lunar Phases

- **New Moon**: Start a new ritual or habit
- **Full Moon**: Celebrate a milestone with a hemp fire ceremony
- **Mercury Retrograde**: Double hemp for clarity and slow integration
- **Saturn Return**: Use consistent hemp rituals for structure and inner stability

◈ *Pro Tip:* Keep a **"Hemp Ritual Log"** that tracks how each blend affects your body, sleep, mood, and spiritual insight. Over time, you'll build a ritual database perfectly suited to your chart.

◈ **Sample Ritual Pairings by Sign**

Sign	Morning Ritual	Evening Ritual
Aries	Energizing hemp matcha + workout affirmations	Smoke ritual + CBD balm for tight muscles
Taurus	Grounding tea + body scan meditation	Hemp foot soak + sensual oils + breathwork
Gemini	Journaling + hemp-infused clarity tea	Storytelling or creative writing with CBD vape
Cancer	Gentle yoga + CBD tincture and prayer	Salt bath + moon journaling
Leo	Mirror affirmations + citrus CBD oil	Candlelit smoke ritual + reflective playlist
Virgo	Planning journal + capsule supplement	Herbal tea with hemp honey + stretching
Libra	Facial massage with hemp + tarot pull	Aesthetic bath + soft music and edibles
Scorpio	Breathwork + deep tea journaling	Shadow journaling + smoke ritual + stillness

Sign	Morning Ritual	Evening Ritual
Sagittarius	Movement + sunrise mantra	Hemp snack + stargazing + dream intentions
Capricorn	Time block ritual + morning supplement	Weighted blanket + balm massage + stillness
Aquarius	Sound ritual + eye-opening CBD blend	Hemp smoke + moon-gazing + creative project
Pisces	Dream recall journaling + mugwort blend	Oil massage + silence + binaural beats

◈ In Summary: A Ritual Life Is a Magical Life

Your body is a constellation. Your breath is a prayer. Your habits are spells.

By crafting **personalized hemp rituals**, you not only enhance physical wellness—you **cultivate a lifestyle of conscious presence**.

Let the stars guide your rhythm. Let hemp ground your practice.

Chapter 14: Spiritual Integration — Astrology, Hemp, and Higher Consciousness

Explore the intersection of metaphysical growth, altered states of consciousness, and spiritual healing. Ideal for those seeking transformation through hemp-enhanced practices.

At the heart of every spiritual journey lies the desire to remember who we truly are. Beneath the identities, titles, and traumas, we are cosmic beings—fragments of the infinite—capable of great healing, deep knowing, and divine creation. The sacred tools of **astrology** and **hemp** have long been used to access this remembrance. When combined intentionally, they form a **bridge between the physical and the metaphysical**, between the body and the soul.

This chapter is for those who are ready to explore **higher consciousness**—to move beyond passive stargazing and wellness routines into **active spiritual evolution**. Through **ritual, altered states, vibrational alignment, and planetary guidance**, we will explore how hemp can become not just a healing aid, but a **portal to transcendence**.

◈ The Soul's Blueprint: Astrology as the Map of Awakening

Your natal chart is more than a personality analysis—it is a **map of the soul's curriculum**. Every planet, every aspect, every transit is a coded message for your personal evolution.

- **Sun Sign**: Your spiritual radiance and core frequency
- **Moon Sign**: Your inner world and emotional karma
- **Rising Sign**: Your chosen path for growth in this incarnation
- **North Node**: Your soul's destiny and dharma
- **Chiron**: Your wounded healer—where your deepest wound becomes your greatest gift

◈ *Spiritual Tip:* Meditate with your birth chart as a **sacred text**. Use a hemp-infused tea or oil to soften resistance and allow insight to rise from within.

◈ **Hemp and Altered States: A Gentle Key to Inner Realms**
Unlike psychedelic substances that shock the system into revelation, hemp offers a **softer, sustainable path** to altered states of consciousness. Its natural compounds—like **CBD, CBN, and terpene profiles**—help **quiet the analytical mind** and **enhance access to intuitive states**.

Hemp supports spiritual growth by:

* **Reducing egoic chatter**, allowing inner wisdom to surface
* **Soothing the nervous system**, so that the soul may speak
* **Enhancing meditation**, visualization, and lucid dreaming
* **Deepening embodiment**, crucial for integrated spiritual work

◈ *Ritual Tip:* Light a candle under a planetary hour (e.g., Jupiter hour for wisdom). Take a calming hemp blend and meditate on your third eye or heart chakra. Ask: "What truth am I ready to receive?"

⬦ Planetary Consciousness and Spiritual Lessons

Each planet represents not just outer influences, but **states of consciousness** that must be integrated over a lifetime.

Planet	Spiritual Theme	Hemp Ritual Idea
Sun	Divine Identity	Solar-charged hemp oil massage for radiance
Moon	Intuition, Sacred Feminine	CBD bath under moonlight with dream journal
Mercury	Thought as Prayer	Hemp tea + automatic writing session
Venus	Love as a Frequency	Heart chakra hemp balm + rose petal altar
Mars	Sacred Will	Grounding smoke blend before releasing ritual
Jupiter	Cosmic Wisdom	Guided journey with hemp + planetary chanting
Saturn	Spiritual Discipline	Hemp salve + ritual journaling of karmic cycles
Uranus	Soul Awakening	Electric meditation with hemp + sound therapy

Planet	Spiritual Theme	Hemp Ritual Idea
Neptune	Mystical Union	Blue lotus + hemp tea for spiritual downloads
Pluto	Death and Rebirth	Shadow work ritual with smoke and candle magic

◈♀ Practices for Expanding Consciousness with Hemp

1. Hemp-Enhanced Meditation

- Choose a blend that includes calming terpenes (myrcene, linalool).
- Meditate with a planetary focus (e.g., Moon on Mondays).
- Use breathwork to guide awareness through your body's energy centers.

2. Astro-Journaling for Soul Growth

- Ingest a calming edible or tincture.
- Use prompts based on current transits (e.g., What is Mercury retrograde teaching me about my truth?)
- Let your hand write freely, inviting downloads from higher self or guides.

3. Smoke Offerings and Rituals

- Create a sacred space with herbs like lavender, hemp, frankincense, or mugwort.
- Light the blend with gratitude.
- Use the smoke as a visual representation of release or spiritual ascent.

4. Dreamwork and Lucid Access

- Take CBN-forward or myrcene-heavy hemp 30 minutes before sleep.
- Place an amethyst or moonstone by your bed.
- Keep a journal to record visions, dreams, and night messages.

◈ Signs of Spiritual Integration

You know you are integrating higher consciousness—not just visiting it—when:

- You respond instead of react
- You honor your emotions without drowning in them
- You feel the cosmic rhythm in your body and choices
- You treat your ritual as a conversation with the divine
- You accept that growth includes discomfort, but not chaos

◈ *Integration Tip:* Use hemp not to escape, but to *deepen*. Make it part of your daily temple—not a retreat from life, but a reconnection to it.

◈ Spiritual Awakening Is a Cycle, Not a Destination

Just as the Moon waxes and wanes, so too does our consciousness expand, contract, and expand again. Hemp is not the answer—it is a **companion**. Astrology is not a belief—it is a **language**. Together, they help us remember who we are and **why we incarnated**.

The path to higher consciousness is not about floating away—it is about anchoring your divine self into your human life.

◈ In Summary: The Sacred Triad of Mind, Plant, and Cosmos

When you pair astrology with intentional hemp use, you walk a path of remembrance.

When you use ritual to return to that path, again and again, you awaken.

Let this chapter be your permission to explore, to deepen, to dissolve old limits, and to rise into the full expression of your cosmic self.

Chapter 15: Living Cosmically — Daily Integration Practices

This final chapter weaves everything together. Learn how to incorporate cosmic timing into everyday decisions, routines, and wellness planning with hemp at your side.

The journey through *Astrological Hemp* has taken you through the stars and back to the soil—tracing a sacred connection between celestial wisdom and earth-grown medicine. As we arrive at this final chapter, the question becomes: **How do we live this wisdom every day?** How do we bring the stars into our schedule, the planets into our planning, and the soul of hemp into our habits?

Living cosmically is not about perfection. It is about presence. It means making choices in alignment with your energy, the lunar and solar cycles, and the deeper flow of your personal astrological blueprint. When we integrate this awareness into the micro-decisions of our lives—what we eat, when we rest, how we reflect—we unlock **wellness that is sustainable, sacred, and self-led**.

This chapter provides **daily, weekly, and seasonal frameworks** for living in alignment with both the stars and the plant allies that walk beside us. You will learn how to build a **cosmic calendar**, structure your rituals, and turn even mundane acts into mindful moments with hemp as your herbal anchor.

◈ The Core Philosophy of Daily Cosmic Living

To live cosmically is to embrace a rhythm beyond the 9–5 clock. It's a **reclaiming of time** as a sacred current that flows with the cosmos—not against it.

Daily cosmic living asks:

- What is the **Moon** doing today?
- What zodiac season are we in?
- Is Mercury retrograde or Saturn exacting?
- How does my **body** feel in relation to the sky's dance?
- What hemp ally supports this phase of life or this planetary lesson?

This doesn't mean obsessing over every degree of a chart—it means **synchronizing your lifestyle with energetic windows** that are already influencing you, whether you're aware of them or not.

◈ **Morning Cosmic Alignment Practice**

Objective: Start the day tuned into your energy, astrology, and intention.

1. **Check the Moon Sign and Phase:**
   Use a lunar calendar or app to note the Moon's current sign and phase. Reflect on how that energy resonates with you today.
2. **Hemp Infusion:**
   - *Waxing Moon:* Sativa hemp tea or oil to build momentum
   - *Waning Moon:* CBD-rich or grounding blend to clear and reset
3. **Astro-Journal Prompt:**
   "Today, under the [Moon Sign] Moon, I feel called to…"
   Write one intention or goal that supports the current cosmic flow.
4. **Movement or Stillness:**
   Air/Fire days = activate with breathwork or a walk
   Earth/Water days = stretch, journal, or meditate
5. **Daily Affirmation Based on Your Sun/Rising Sign**

◈ *Example for Scorpio Moon in Pisces Season:*

- Hemp oil dropper under the tongue
- Quiet meditation with ocean sounds
- Intention: "Today I honor emotional flow and release what clings."

◈ Weekly Planning with Planetary Days

Each day of the week carries planetary energy. Align your planning and hemp use accordingly:

Day	Planet	Themes	Hemp Support
Monday	Moon	Emotions, rest, reflection	Soothing tea, dream tinctures
Tuesday	Mars	Action, courage, motivation	Energizing strain or capsule
Wednesday	Mercury	Communication, learning	Focus-enhancing edible or oil
Thursday	Jupiter	Expansion, gratitude, growth	Journaling + joy-infused tea
Friday	Venus	Beauty, love, art	Topicals, facial oil, aroma
Saturday	Saturn	Structure, boundaries	Ritual bath, grounding oil
Sunday	Sun	Vitality, radiance, rest	Solar-charged balm, outdoor time

◈ *Tip:* Build your **self-care planner** around this rhythm. Allow flexibility but prioritize ritual consistency.

◈ **Monthly and Seasonal Wellness Strategy**

Just as nature changes with the seasons, so should your **hemp rituals and cosmic planning**. Each zodiac season highlights a body part, life lesson, and type of healing.

◈ **Monthly Check-In:**

- What zodiac season are we in? (e.g., Leo = heart, joy, boldness)
- What upcoming **retrogrades**, **eclipses**, or **new/full moons** are scheduled?
- Which body systems or chakras need support this month?

◈ **Seasonal Ritual Shift Example:**

Aries Season (Spring Equinox):

- Action-based hemp blends
- Fire rituals, planning bold goals
- Physical detox + cardio-based movement

Libra Season (Fall Equinox):

- Heart-opening hemp oils
- Relationship reflection journaling
- Balance-focused yoga and tea rituals

◈ Cosmic Integration Toolkit: Essential Practices

1. **Daily Moon Check-In**
   - Ask: "How can I flow with the Moon today?"
   - Track moods and rituals in a lunar journal.
2. **Astro-Hemp Cabinet**
   - Curate blends by element (e.g., fiery for Leo, watery for Pisces)
   - Label hemp products with associated signs and phases
3. **Sacred Sunday Review**
   - Reflect on your past week through a cosmic lens
   - Identify stress points, wins, and patterns
   - Reset with a hemp bath or oil massage
4. **Cosmic Vision Board**
   - Use zodiac houses to map life areas (2nd = money, 7th = love)
   - Place hemp-infused symbols (leaves, oils, affirmations) by each section

◈ Living Cosmically in a Modern World

Cosmic living is **not about escaping modern life**, but bringing sacredness *into it*.

It's the moment you infuse your coffee with gratitude, choose your to-do list based on moon cycles, or take a CBD break because you know Saturn is demanding too much today.

It's the quiet wisdom of *asking the sky what your soul already knows*—and letting the earth's plant allies, like hemp, help you act on it.

◇ **Final Thought: A Life Aligned**

You are no longer separate from the cosmos—you are an expression of it.

You are no longer a consumer of wellness—you are the **architect of your alignment**.

Let *Astrological Hemp* be your ongoing guide as you weave intention into every breath, drop, ritual, and choice. From the soil to the stars, your healing is in your hands.

You don't need to live perfectly.

Just **live consciously**.

Appendix A: Glossary of Astrological & Hemp Terms

Key definitions to support cosmic literacy and plant-based wellness integration.

◈ Astrological Terms

Astrology — The ancient study of celestial bodies and their influence on human life, personality, emotions, and world events. Astrology is both a symbolic language and a timing tool.

Zodiac — A circle of twelve 30-degree sections along the ecliptic, each representing an archetypal energy (sign). The signs are: Aries, Taurus, Gemini, Cancer, Leo, Virgo, Libra, Scorpio, Sagittarius, Capricorn, Aquarius, Pisces.

Natal Chart (Birth Chart) — A map of the sky at the exact moment of your birth, showing the positions of the planets, the Sun, and the Moon. It reveals your energetic blueprint.

Sun Sign — The zodiac sign the Sun was in at your birth. Represents core identity, vitality, and conscious ego.

Moon Sign — The sign the Moon occupied at your birth. Governs emotional nature, subconscious, and comfort zones.

Rising Sign (Ascendant) — The sign rising on the eastern horizon at your time of birth. Represents your outward personality and life path.

Planets — Celestial bodies that symbolize different forces in the psyche:

- **Mercury**: Communication, thought
- **Venus**: Love, beauty, attraction
- **Mars**: Drive, aggression, will
- **Jupiter**: Expansion, wisdom
- **Saturn**: Discipline, responsibility
- **Uranus**: Innovation, awakening
- **Neptune**: Dreams, illusions
- **Pluto**: Transformation, power

Houses — Twelve divisions in the natal chart that represent different areas of life (e.g., self, money, relationships, career).

Aspects — The angles formed between planets in the chart that indicate harmony or tension:

- **Conjunction (0°)** – Merged energies
- **Sextile (60°)** – Cooperative flow
- **Square (90°)** – Challenge, friction
- **Trine (120°)** – Easy harmony
- **Opposition (180°)** – Tension between extremes

Modalities — How signs act:

- **Cardinal**: Initiators (Aries, Cancer, Libra, Capricorn)
- **Fixed**: Stabilizers (Taurus, Leo, Scorpio, Aquarius)
- **Mutable**: Adapters (Gemini, Virgo, Sagittarius, Pisces)

Elements — The fundamental energetic nature of signs:

- **Fire** (Aries, Leo, Sagittarius): Passion, action
- **Earth** (Taurus, Virgo, Capricorn): Stability, embodiment
- **Air** (Gemini, Libra, Aquarius): Thought, communication
- **Water** (Cancer, Scorpio, Pisces): Emotion, intuition

Retrograde — When a planet appears to move backward in the sky. Energetically, it represents internal reflection, revision, or disruption of its usual domain (e.g., Mercury retrograde = miscommunication).

Moon Phases —

- **New Moon**: Intention-setting, beginnings
- **Waxing Moon**: Building momentum
- **Full Moon**: Illumination, climax
- **Waning Moon**: Release, rest

Chiron — An asteroid known as the "Wounded Healer." Shows where your deepest emotional wounds can become your greatest healing gifts.

Nodes (North & South) — Points that indicate soul purpose (North Node) and past life patterns or karmic tendencies (South Node).

Transits — The current movement of planets and how they interact with your natal chart, triggering growth or challenge.

◇ Hemp & Wellness Terms

Hemp — A strain of the cannabis plant bred to contain less than 0.3% THC. Non-psychoactive and legal in many countries, hemp is used for wellness, textiles, food, and spiritual ritual.

Cannabis — A plant genus that includes both marijuana (high THC) and hemp (low THC). While genetically similar, the legal definitions depend on THC content.

CBD (Cannabidiol) — A non-psychoactive cannabinoid found in hemp known for its calming, anti-inflammatory, and anxiolytic effects. Promotes balance without getting "high."

THC (Tetrahydrocannabinol) — The psychoactive compound in cannabis that produces a "high." Present in low amounts in hemp (<0.3%).

CBN (Cannabinol) — A minor cannabinoid known for its sedative and sleep-promoting qualities, often used in hemp sleep products.

Full-Spectrum — Hemp extract containing all cannabinoids, terpenes, flavonoids, and trace THC. Offers an "entourage effect" where compounds work synergistically.

Broad-Spectrum — Similar to full-spectrum but with **no THC**. Retains most of the hemp plant's benefits while being THC-free.

Isolate — A purified extract that contains only one compound, usually CBD. No other cannabinoids or terpenes are present.

Terpenes — Aromatic compounds found in hemp and many plants. They influence flavor, scent, and therapeutic effects.

- **Linalool**: Calming (also found in lavender)
- **Myrcene**: Sedative and relaxing
- **Limonene**: Uplifting and citrusy
- **Pinene**: Alertness and memory boost
- **Caryophyllene**: Anti-inflammatory and grounding

Endocannabinoid System (ECS) — A biological system in humans and animals responsible for maintaining balance (homeostasis) across mood, pain, immunity, and sleep. Hemp compounds interact directly with ECS receptors (CB1 & CB2).

Bioavailability — The degree and rate at which a substance is absorbed and becomes active in the body. Different hemp forms (oils, capsules, smoke, edibles) have varying bioavailability.

Psychoactive — Substances that affect the mind. CBD is **non-psychoactive**, while THC is **psychoactive**.

Ritual Use — The intentional use of hemp in spiritual or wellness practices, often paired with meditation, lunar cycles, or energy healing.

Sativa vs. Indica (in hemp context) — While true hemp strains don't induce highs, **sativa-dominant** strains may offer uplifted or energizing effects, while **indica-dominant** may provide deeper calm or sleep support.

Carrier Oils — Oils like MCT, hempseed, or olive oil used to dilute and deliver cannabinoids in tinctures and topicals.

Entourage Effect — The synergistic effect of using multiple plant compounds (cannabinoids + terpenes + flavonoids) for enhanced benefits.

◈ Conclusion: The Language of Stars and Plants

This glossary is not just a reference—it's a **lexicon for empowerment**. The more fluently you speak the language of the cosmos and the Earth, the more precise and intuitive your healing practices become.

Let this appendix be your guidebook as you build daily rituals, deepen your understanding, and share this wisdom with others.